HUMAN ANGELS

365 Wisdom Pills

*Your daily dose
of Angelic Wisdom*

© 2012 Human Angels
ISBN-13: 978-1500878443
ISBN-10: 1500878448

Text revision: Ross Wilkins
wilkins.ross@rocketmail.com

Cover design: Roberto De Gregorio
degraf@tin.it

To our joyous angel Medora

*Thanks to our Angels
for having inspired us to write this book.
May you receive support and faith
from these angelic words of wisdom
and, through them, remember
the wonderful, Divine being that is You.*

Our beloved Angels have inspired us to write this book that contains 365 simple, yet profound Pills of Wisdom with the purpose of giving you faith, support and instant help for your spiritual growth.

The journey towards the Consciousness that we are all One is sometimes difficult with pitfalls created by our egos to keep us glued to our old beliefs.

During this journey, you might sometimes feel lost and lonely, searching for help and inspiration. In this case, *"365 Wisdom Pills"* is the remedy that, providing you with a daily dose of angelic wisdom, will strengthen you and jump-start your healing process.

"365 Wisdom Pills" also has positive and long-lasting effects on your spiritual health and self-worth, making you able to heal yourself from the emotional wounds that have caused suffering in your life.

Please read all of the following leaflet carefully, before you start taking the Wisdom Pills.

Wisdom Pills Leaflet

The *Wisdom Pills* are recommended to start the healing process, from small to large emotional wounds and to reawaken the highest potential of every human being: their Divine Nature, the inner Human Angel that is waiting to be activated by the bright light of Consciousness. Their positive effects are immediate and evident.

1. What Wisdom Pills are
The *Wisdom Pills* contain the active substance called "Soul Consciousness". This substance works directly on the soul to help you feel more self-confident, relaxed and joyful.

2. How Wisdom Pills work
The *Wisdom Pills* act on those parts of yourself (suffering of the past, illusion of

fear and self-destructive feelings) that need to be brought into balance. You are permitted to pass it on to others if their "symptoms" are the same as yours.

3. What the Wisdom Pills are used for
You have chosen to take the *Wisdom Pills* in order to heal your life and achieve a brighter state of Angelic Wisdom. *"365 Wisdom Pills"* will give you a new, enlightened perspective on your entire life.

4. How to take the Wisdom Pills
You can take as many pills as you like from the beginning of the treatment, although it is recommended that you start with just a few pills a day in order to enable the active substance contained within the medicine to have the full effect on your soul.

5. Possible side effects
The *Wisdom Pills* also have a positive effect on the heart, opening it up to greater love and compassion, due to the restorative action of forgiveness.

6. Warnings and precautions
If you take more Wisdom Pills than is recommended
There are absolutely no risks or contraindications if you take too many pills per day.
If you forget to take Wisdom Pills
Do not worry: the positive effects of *Wisdom Pills* are long lasting, and you will be able to recall, from memory, the previous pills that you have already taken, because their effect has no end.

7. How to store Wisdom Pills
Always Keep *Wisdom Pills* with you, as an ebook it does not take too much space. As a paperback, the light weight and small size makes it easy to carry with you at all times.

Marketing Authorization Holder and Manufacturer
Human Angels, Mother Earth, Oneness
Facebook: We Are Human Angels
Twitter: @HUMAN_ANGELS
Website: www.wearehumanangels.com

365
Wisdom Pills

1

*Ego judges and punishes.
Love forgives and heals.*

2

*We do not need to learn anything,
because our souls
already know everything.
To learn means to remember.*

3

*The recipe for abundance is:
love yourself, be grateful
and let the Universe work for you.*

4

*When we hurt someone else,
we hurt ourselves.
When we love someone else,
we love ourselves.
In the Oneness, every action
belongs to everyone.*

5

*Sometimes we can
communicate more
by being silent than talking.
Sometimes we can do more
by doing nothing
than trying to do something.*

6

*When you are at peace
with your past,
you are at peace with yourself.*

7

*What is visible is impermanent,
what is invisible is permanent.*

8

*Happiness doesn't come
from expensive things, it comes
from living ones own passions.*

9

*By living in the present,
you heal your past and your future.*

10

*Only the total and unconditional
acceptance of yourself makes you able
to love and to be loved by others.*

11

The less you judge, the more you love.

12

Living with faith creates heaven on earth.

13

Forgiveness frees the forgiver.

14

*To live in harmony with oneself
is the basis of a wonderful life.*

15

When you follow your passions,

you never get lost.

16

*The language of the heart is a universal language with no boundaries.
The language of the heart never changes.
The language of the heart can be understood by everyone, everywhere.*

17

*What belongs to time,
disappears with time.
What belongs to the Spirit
is forever.*

18

*We are all One.
We all come from the same Source
of Love and Light.*

19

*A failure becomes a victory
when we learn from it.*

20

*A lack of respect for others
is also a lack of self-respect.*

21

*Forgiveness is the key
that unlocks the heart.*

22

*Whatever you do
to make things happen,
everything happens at the perfect time.*

23

B*y forgiving, you let go of your past
and allow your future to arrive.*

24

*Unconditional love energy
is our divine heritage.*

25

W*hen we recognize our Divine Nature,
we understand that fear
is an illusion created by our minds.*

26

*Everything is possible
in the name of Love, even miracles.*

27

Self-acceptance doesn't mean
that we stop trying to improve ourselves,
it does mean that we value
and unconditionally love ourselves.

28

Heaven is
a state of consciousness.

29

Love is the cause, the meaning
and the purpose of everything.

30

Peace and bliss
can be found in the space
of emptiness within oneself.

31

*What we see in our physical reality,
is only a small part of what we really are.*

32

*Everything you think
you need to learn, you already know.
Everything you are looking for,
you have already found.*

33

*Love is joy: the joy of giving
and the joy of receiving.*

34

*Here and Now
is the endless beauty
of every moment of life.*

35

I Am:
this is the magic formula
that will transform your life.

36

Truth is what is sleeping
within you, wake it up.

37

The meaning of life
is found in every moment of living,
the meaning of life is life itself.

38

A problem is a problem
only when you think it is a problem.
In the perspective of your soul,

*every problem is an opportunity
to achieve a higher consciousness.*

39

*Forgiveness cannot change your past,
but can heal your present.*

40

*Unconditional Love in the Oneness
is our highest fulfillment.*

41

*The All is contained
in your inner center of consciousness.*

42

By losing your fears, you find yourself.

43

*When you do not judge yourself,
you become able
to freely express your feelings.*

44

*When Love reigns,
miracles become normality.*

45

*Lack of love is an illusion, be aware
of all the Love that already surrounds you.*

46

*The practice of Unconditional Love
starts with the full acceptance
of yourself, just as you are.*

47

*Even if the truth makes you
uncomfortable, always seek it.*

48

*When you feel love within,
you feel love all around.*

49

*Love is
the never-ending energy of Life.*

50

*By forgiving yourself,
you regain your lost innocence
and the joy of living.*

51

*When your intention is pure,
your action will be just.*

52

*You cannot help anybody
who doesn't want to be helped.
You are not responsible
for the destiny of others.
Souls choose their journey according
to the Sacred Law of Free Will.
Just bless everyone and their path.*

53

*When your mind is silent, you can listen
to your heart and remember that
everything is Love and you are that Love.*

54

*The higher we go, the further we fall:
this is how we learn to fly.*

55

*To think doesn't bring us any answers.
To love brings all the answers.*

56

*When Life is asking us to change,
we have two choices:
feeling the pain of the end
or feeling the joy of a new beginning.*

57

When ego disappears, Oneness appears.

58

*The key to achieving
Unconditional Love is to stop judging.*

59

*The ultimate measure
of Consciousness is Integrity.*

60

*Human beings, projecting themselves,
have created a judging God,
because they always judge
themselves and others.
But God is Unconditional Love,
that is Love without judgment.*

61

In the Oneness, we release the feeling

*of being less than or more than,
in the Oneness everyone
is unique and equal.*

62

*Every time that a human being
feels Unconditional Love,
this planet becomes a better place.*

63

*Life is a mystery
that can be understood through the heart
and not through the mind.*

64

*Every time
we overcome our suffering,
we open our hearts
to a greater compassion.*

65

*Dreams, Vision and Free Will
make everything possible.*

66

*Unconditional Love
is the only freedom from attachment.*

67

*In order to totally release your past
and to move forward,
you have first to go back.
Accept this as a blessed healing opportunity.*

68

*Every grain of sand
is different from any other grain of sand*

in the rest of the Uni-verse.

69

*What you seek is what you find.
What you find is what you seek.*

70

*When we look at our lives
through the eyes of the mind,
our vision is limited and incomplete.
When we look through the eyes
of the Heart, we become One
with what we are looking at.*

71

*When we judge,
we deny the Oneness.
When we love unconditionally,
we join the Oneness.*

72

*Those that look for happiness,
never find it.
Those that look for oneself,
find happiness.*

73

*Nobody can hurt you,
if you first don't hurt yourself.
Nobody can betray you,
if you first don't betray yourself.
Nobody can truly be in love with you,
if you are first not in love with yourself.*

74

*Rules come from
the mind and judgment.
Values come from the heart,
because of this, love has no rules,
love only has values.*

75

*A thankful heart
is the key to overflowing joy.*

76

*Fill your heart
with beauty everyday.*

77

*The feeling of Oneness
is the feeling of Heaven.*

78

*We are Light,
powerful rays of Light,
from a unique Source.*

79

*Unconditional acceptance
is the key to open
the door of awareness.*

80

*When Love leads our steps,
we never get lost.*

81

*All is One,
everything is connected to everything.*

82

*Every day is a wonderful surprise,
when we stop having the illusion
of control over the flow of life.*

83

*Love is not blind, Love sees very well.
Love sees through the eyes of the heart.*

84

*Stop thinking
what is right and what is wrong:
rely on the perfection of the Oneness.*

85

*One by one we can
change our own world,
all together we can create
Heaven on earth.*

86

Things simply happen:

*those that stay out of judgment,
stay out of suffering.*

87

T*o know is to love.
To love is to know.*

88

I*n Unconditional Love,
there are no pretensions
and expectations.
Leaving others free to give,
what we receive is always
an unexpected gift for our open hearts.*

89

E*mpty your mind
and fill your heart with the infinite
Bliss of the Oneness.*

90

*You are never more alive
than when you follow your passions.*

91

*Complaining about misfortune
never brings awareness.
Accepting it with confidence
always brings awareness.*

92

*Breathing the silence,
you can listen to your heart.*

93

*Forgiveness dries your tears
and frees your heart.*

94

*Fear is limiting, Love expands.
Because of this the Uni-verse is infinite.*

95

True greatness belongs to humble people.

96

*We are all One
and Love is what we truly are.*

97

*By changing our inner world,
we change the world.*

98

*Every time
you feel unworthy of love,
remember that you are
the perfect child of God,
created by love to love.*

99

*Past and future are the time of ego.
Here and Now is the time of the Oneness.*

100

*Nothing can really change your life:
meditation, success, spiritual practices.
Nobody can really save you: a guru,
a friend, a new love.
Only you can do it for yourself.*

101

*Unconditional love
is a flower that blooms forever.*

102

B*illions of people,
billions of souls, billions of stars,
only one Truth: the Oneness.*

103

B*e thankful to your life
for all the love you have
received and given.*

104

B*e compassionate, forgive yourself.*

105

Peace is the outcome of forgiveness.

106

*Negative emotions and thoughts
nourish illness.
Love nourishes health.*

107

*When you grow in consciousness,
you also grow in love.*

108

*Those that have all but do not have
joy in the heart, have nothing.
Those that have joy in the heart,
have everything.*

109

*The practice of Unconditional Love
is the way to Oneness.*

110

*Whatever you have done,
nothing can spoil the purity
of your divine nature.*

111

*The heart is the master.
The heart is the measure of all things.*

112

*Life always flows.
By trying to hold on to what you know,
you limit your possibility to experience*

the joy of the present moment.

113

***D**etachment is the secret
of ultimate happiness.*

114

***I**f you want to find love, stop seeking it.*

115

***W**hen your past stops being a burden
it becomes a source of inner richness.*

116

***S**ynchronicity is the sign
that you are in the flow.*

117

*The more you share,
the more you feel joy in your heart.*

118

*In the whole universe,
there is no one else exactly like you.
You are an unrepeatable miracle of Love.*

119

*Those that do not learn
from the sufferings of the past,
will continue to face similar trials
until they consciously decide to turn their
sufferings into Awareness and Love.*

120

If hope is the last to die, faith never dies.

121

*True love is unconditional,
true forgiveness is unconditional,
true acceptance is unconditional.*

122

Awareness is freedom.

123

*By taking responsibility
for your life and your happiness,
you overcome your victim mentality
and step into the power
of your spiritual mastery.*

124

*Pride is a prison.
Humility is freedom.*

125

True love conquers fear.

126

*Everyday everywhere
with everyone, plant seeds of love.
Love is the only revolution
that can really change the world.*

127

*Weaknesses are nothing
to be ashamed of.
By accepting and not by hiding them,
weaknesses become a source of strength.*

128

*Treat everyone
as the Divine Beings that they are.*

*Treat yourself
as the Divine Being that you Are.*

129

***O**neness is
what you always are,
even when you believe
in the illusion of separation.*

130

***L**ove
makes your life blossom.*

131

***E**nlightenment is something
that spontaneously happens
when you choose to fulfill
your highest potential.*

132

Always love with respect.

133

*Life is what everyone does
with their infinite potential.*

134

*Your mistakes have helped you
to become a better person.*

135

*Judging and criticizing others
is an exhausting job.
Loving others unconditionally
is an infinite pleasure.*

136

*Enduring happiness comes
from sharing our blessings with others.*

137

*Do not ask your mind
to solve your problems,
the solution is already written
in the wisdom of your heart.*

138

*Sometimes the truth may hurt,
but it always heals.*

139

*The more you try to run away
from your fears,
the greater the fears become.*

140

*For every effect in your life,
there is a cause. And the cause
is always within oneself.*

141

*In everything you do,
be Love.*

142

*When you surrender
your problems to the flow of life,
solutions spontaneously come.*

143

*Love is the best gift
that you can give or receive.*

144

*Be happy now.
You do not need to achieve anything
to feel happy:
endless happiness is your true nature.*

145

*Compassion arises when you start
to understand the sorrows of others,
without judging them.*

146

*Unconditional Love is Divine Eternal Love:
it endures despite all circumstances
and it lasts forever.*

147

When your inner light shines,

you become a star in the universe.

148

***B**ehind great anger, there is great fear.*

149

***O**nly when you forgive yourself,
can you allow yourself to be
worthy of love and happiness.*

150

***E**veryone who is part of your life,
is a part of you.*

151

***G**enerosity generates abundance.*

152

*Love comes into your life,
only when you allow it to come.*

153

*You never waste your time,
when you are learning
to love yourself.*

154

*Every separation is illusion,
everything is connected
in the Oneness.*

155

*The more love you give,
the more love you have to give.*

156

*Every moment is unique,
never before, never again.
Enjoy your life.*

157

*When you feel sad,
desperate and hopeless,
remember: the darkest hour
comes just before the dawn.*

158

New awareness clears old problems.

159

*Everything is energy.
Everything is Love.*

160

*Root yourself into the earth
and you will rise to the stars.*

161

*Be master of your own destiny,
not a slave to your past.*

162

*Silence is golden,
in the pure silence of the mind
is hidden the treasure of Being.*

163

*In the universal mind, everything
that exists has always existed
and always will exist.*

164

*Those that plant seeds of Love
will live a flourishing life.*

165

*Accept that changes
create loss and separation.
Accept that your life is
a journey into the unknown
full of wonderful surprises.*

166

Given love is returned multiplied.

167

*Being true is the best way
to attract the best life for oneself.*

168

*In your darkest moments,
start to count the countless reasons
you have to be grateful in your life.*

169

*Faith is not what you believe,
faith is how you live.*

170

*Miracles happen
when we allow love
to flow freely into our lives.*

171

*When you start loving yourself,
you stop losing yourself*

*when loving someone else:
you learn how to love
without losing your self-respect.*

172

*Do not ever forget
that you are special and unique.
Treat yourself as you deserve.*

173

*Through your inner peace,
you can bring peace to the world.*

174

*Pride inhibits the freedom
to be emotional, to be fragile
and to be authentic.*

175

*Feel humble, be humble
and live for greatness.*

176

*The outcome of every action
depends on the intention behind the action.*

177

*Believing in oneself
is the secret to succeed in everything.*

178

*In the world of duality,
you can choose to love or not to love.
In the Oneness, Love is the only choice.*

179

*Sometimes,
telling the truth
is one of the hardest things to do,
but it is also one of the best things
to do for oneself.*

180

*You stop being worried
when you surrender
to the loving flow of life.*

181

*Abundance only has meaning
when shared,
joy only has meaning
when shared,
awareness only has meaning
when shared.*

182

*Live as if you were
to die tomorrow.
Live as if you will never die.*

183

*We are always the most implacable
judges of ourselves, until
we learn to unconditionally love ourselves.*

184

*Share the Divine with everyone
you encounter in your life:
this is the most precious thing
you can share.*

185

Be tolerant even when you meet

*someone who gives you
unpleasant feelings.
Tolerance is part of
Unconditional Love.*

186

*When we project positiveness,
positiveness is what
we receive back.*

187

*Love your weaknesses,
you can learn a lot from them.*

188

*Everything loses its meaning
in the Oneness.
Everything only has meaning
in the Oneness.*

189

*Live simply, live happily,
live a compassionate life.*

190

*Events in our lives are nothing
but what our souls have chosen
in order to let go of duality
and return to the Oneness.*

191

*A great loss is a painful illusion.
In your soul nothing is ever lost.*

192

*Every separation is an illusion.
We are all fragments
of the Oneness of Love.*

193

*The fears that you
do not face today,
will come back tomorrow.*

194

*Forgiveness is
the only antidote
for poisoned hearts.*

195

*We are Oneness having
the experience of duality.*

196

*There is nothing more joyful
than Unconditional Love,
there is nothing more peaceful*

*than Unconditional Love,
there is nothing bigger
than Unconditional Love.*

197

*Take a break
from the noise of the world
and listen to the powerful
sound of silence.*

198

*Stop looking for happiness
and let happiness find you.*

199

*When you are connected
with the Source of all good,
all good becomes available to you.*

200

*When you change something
within yourself,
things will spontaneously
change in your life.*

201

Don't fear fear, just breathe.

202

*The quality of your life
doesn't depend on the quality
of what you have, it depends
on the quality of your feelings.*

203

When you do not know what to do,

*do nothing, wait with confidence
and everything spontaneously happens.*

204

*Everything can be good and bad
at the same time, when we are living
in a relative world.
Everything is always perfect,
when we are living
in the world of Oneness.*

205

*To laugh,
just for the pleasure of laughing,
is a sign of wisdom.*

206

*The origin of everything is
the Void filled by Divine Love.*

207

*A winner is someone
who is able to learn
from their failures
and never gives up.*

208

*We cannot know love
if we first have not experienced it.
We cannot know the Truth
if we first have not experienced it.*

209

*Your destiny
is not already written.
You are, in every moment,
the only author of your book of life.*

210

*Send love and healing energy
to all parts of yourself
that you want to change,
then let love work on them.*

211

*Enlightenment is
the constant feeling of joy,
without any memory of the sorrow
that we felt along the path.*

212

*Send waves of love to the world,
where people are fighting.
The world needs your love.*

213

*The higher the frequency
of your desire raises,
the faster will be the time
for its manifestation.*

214

*Acceptance has nothing
to do with passivity.
Acceptance leads you
to the wisest choices.*

215

*Bless your enemies,
they are in your life to show you
which part of yourself
you need to heal.*

216

*Love, joy and abundance
are like kind guests that
come into your life
only when they are
sincerely invited.*

217

*What you do not accept in others
is what you do not accept
within yourself.
What you love in others is
what you love within yourself.*

218

*An inconvenient truth
is a gift of love*

219

*Your heart is
the sun of your life,
everything exists because of it
and everything revolves around it.*

220

*What you expect, comes
when and how you don't expect it.*

221

Confidence has patience.

222

*When you feel lost
in the waves of life, faith is the rudder
and love is the anchor.*

223

*Resentment is a lack of forgiveness.
When you get rid of resentment,
you get rid of the sorrow of your past.*

224

*You are alive, this is a gift
to live to the fullest.*

225

*Inhale love, exhale love:
love is the breathe of life.*

226

*The ultimate outcome
of unconditional love for oneself
is universal love in the Oneness.*

227

What you believe, you create.

228

*When love is mixed up
with need and attachment,
suffering is the inevitable outcome.*

229

Sow goodness, gather love.

230

*The ego never rests:
when the ego achieves something,
it immediately wants something new,
something different, until its final
surrender to the Oneness.*

231

*Suffering always comes from
the forgetfulness of your Divine Nature.
Simply by remembering the power of
"I Am", you can release all the burden of
suffering and even smile about it.*

232

*The silence of the mind is
the starting point for enlightenment.*

233

*Good and evil, everything
is melted in the Oneness.*

234

Everyone deserves your love.

235

Before taking a decision,
wait until you find the best choice
for you and for all the people
involved in your decision.

236

There is no greater forgiveness
than the forgiveness for oneself.

237

Everywhere you look
you can see yourself in different forms:
this is the Consciousness of Oneness.

238

To love oneself is

*the sweetest remedy when life
has the bitter taste of delusion.*

239

*Only the acceptance of ourselves
makes us able to accept
love from others.*

240

*In order to heal a bad habit,
first heal the mental habit behind it.*

241

*Joy or suffering:
the essence of friendship is,
always and in any case,
sharing without feeling judged.*

242

*By cultivating silence,
you cultivate your spirit.*

243

*Only those that live always
in the Here and Now can be
always present and aware.*

244

*Everything is perfect as it is.
Everything is always perfect
in the Oneness.*

245

*Fear is the forgetting
of our Divine Nature.*

246

*You are the master of your own destiny.
To change it for the better is up to you.*

247

*Feel worthy of your desires,
if you want to make them come true.*

248

*Use the power of the present
to get rid of your past.*

249

*Only when you do not judge others,
can you feel Unconditional Love
and Compassion for them.*

250

By being at peace, you bring peace.

251

If you can dream it, you can achieve it.

252

When somebody has the courage to be oneself, others are encouraged to be themselves.

253

You have, at every moment, the power to overcome your fears by simply remembering your Divine Nature.

254

*Being inspired means to be
an open channel for the Divine Love.*

255

*A lack of contact with nature
is a lack of contact with oneself.*

256

*Compassion only arises
when others' sufferings
are felt with an open heart.*

257

*With little lies, life can be simpler.
With honest words, life can be greater.*

258

*Ego is the mask that,
showing the illusion of separation,
hides the truth of the Oneness.*

259

*Dream, believe, persist
and you'll succeed.*

260

*When the mind is peaceful,
the heart is joyful.*

261

*First make things happen
within yourself, then let things
spontaneously happen in your life.*

262

*Unconditional love is
the memory of our Divine Nature.*

263

*The future is the outcome
of what we think about it.*

264

*What is important is not
what you believe,
it is how you change your life
by virtue of your beliefs.*

265

*The more you love yourself,
the more joyful you become.*

266

*By listening to the heart,
you open your life
to the infinite within yourself.*

267

*Simplicity
and humbleness of heart
are divine wisdom.*

268

*The cure for human suffering
is in the awareness of the Oneness.*

269

*Pain never lasts forever:
you are, at every moment,*

*surrounded by Love
and Love lasts forever.*

270

*Joy in the heart has more value
than all the treasures in the world,
because it is the greatest treasure.*

271

*Suffering is
the outcome of "love" of the ego.
Joy is
the outcome of Unconditional Love.*

272

*Obstacles and problems are warnings,
they show you which parts in your life
need to be brought into balance.*

273

*Live a life with no regrets:
always act with love.*

274

*Welcome every trial
as a blessed opportunity
to overcome your limits,
breaking through the barriers
of self-limitation
in order to fulfill your potential.*

275

*Find your own truth
by following your heart.*

276

Be your own purpose.

277

*A grateful heart
is the secret to a happy life.*

278

*There is no better time
than Now.
There is no other time
than Now.*

279

*The best love is the kind
that frees the heart
and awakens the soul.*

280

*God is not separate
from the material world.*

*God is not separate from you.
God is within you. God is you.*

281

*The ideas of "me" and "mine"
are the seeds of every problem
in the world.*

282

*We love others unconditionally
only when we leave them totally free
to make their own life journey.*

283

*When a great loss seems
to destroy your faith,
this is the time
to keep your heart open
and to feel that the person*

*you lost is always with you.
Continuously talking to you
through signs and through
the universal language of the heart.*

284

Your inner light always shines.

285

*Don't look for Love,
let Love find you.
Don't waste time and energy,
when you are ready,
Love will knock at your door.*

286

*Only when you love yourself,
are you in a condition
to give love to others.*

287

Let Love enlighten your path.

288

*The Divine Spirit of the Oneness
is inherent to everyone
and to everything, with no exceptions.*

289

*When we live in the Here and Now,
at every moment we are reborn to Love.*

290

*The only limits we have
are self imposed.*

291

*Before starting to search
for love in the world,
we have to find love
within ourselves.*

292

*Only when you let go of the old,
can you make room for the new.*

293

*The stronger the faith,
the greater the courage.*

294

Consciousness brings happiness.

295

Don't be afraid of happiness.

296

*The pleasure of sharing
gives meaning
to the blessing of having.*

297

*Suffering comes from
a lack of awareness.
Joy comes from
a plenty of awareness.*

298

The sound of silence

is the voice of the heart.

299

*Synchronicity is how
Universal Love manifests itself
in everybody's life.*

300

*Those that go with the wind
will always be where
it is perfect to be.*

301

*Surrender means
to accept life for what it is
and to stop wasting energy
on swimming against the tide.*

302

*Loving yourself teaches you
how to love others.*

303

B*y healing your past,
you free your future.*

304

I*n the silence of our minds,
listening to ourselves,
we feel that we are never alone,
because we are always connected
with Uni-versal Love.*

305

No one is not better than

*or less than you,
everyone is unique.*

306

*Awareness is
the mind's emptiness.*

307

*By cosmic law, Angels
cannot intervene in human life
without permission, the same law applies
to Human Angels: this is the Sacred Law
of Free Will.*

308

*Self-forgiveness means letting go of
all the feelings of guilt that
we hold against ourselves.*

309

*We are addicted to suffering,
let's start to be addicted to Love.*

310

Beyond the darkness, the Light laughs.

311

*Live a life without expectations,
live every moment to the fullest.*

312

*What happens in our life is nothing
but the result of our inner programming.*

313

*Know your limits but never believe
that they are unbeatable.*

314

*Take your time to love.
Take your time to live.*

315

*Your inner Source is
the ultimate master of wisdom.*

316

*Do not act until
you are able to act with love.*

317

*Everything is possible,
when you believe in yourself.*

318

*Only when you trust yourself,
can you trust others.*

319

*Darkness is an illusion
that disappears with the Light.*

320

*Being able to ask for help is not
a sign of weakness, it is a sign of strength.*

321

*By loving and helping others
without conditions,
you express your angelic nature.*

322

*The Sky is our father.
The Earth is our mother.
In the Oneness, we are all
sisters and brothers of Love.*

323

Love is our eternal essence.

324

World peace starts in everyone's heart.

325

*A life of gratitude is
always blessed
by the grace of God.*

326

*In order to forgive an "offender",
we have first to forgive ourselves,
then we can forgive them.
In this way we are not
helpless victims anymore,
we regain our power,
acting from our peaceful place
of power.*

327

*The truth is within you.
The truth has always
been there.*

328

*Oneness is the only reality.
All the rest is illusion.*

329

*The voice of God
can be heard only
in the inner space of silence.*

330

Love heals, Love is healthy.

331

*As within so without.
Love yourself and you will attract
love into your life.*

332

*Love is not a calculation,
Love is a free gift.*

333

*The secret of life, Love,
is too simple to be understood
by a complicated mind.*

334

*Forgiveness makes your life
lighter and brighter.*

335

*You start peace
by bringing peace to yourself.*

336

*Believe in yourself
and you will see miracles.*

337

*The Love you feel
for others is nothing
but a reflection of the Love
you feel for yourself.*

338

*Your heart can see
what your eyes cannot see.*

339

Unconditional Love lasts forever.

340

*When we believe in our Divine Nature,
our desires become orders of Love
for the Uni-verse.*

341

*Heaven is not somewhere
in the sky, heaven is within you.*

342

*If you pray and if you believe,
you will receive.*

343

*You are the ocean that believes itself
to be a single drop.*

344

*Give thanks
for every single moment of your life:
for your happiest
and your saddest moments.
Whatever happened,
this life's journey has given you
so very much to be grateful for.*

345

*When you forgive,
your suffering becomes
your wealth.*

346

*The path to the Oneness is
the path of your heart.*

347

You are where your heart is.

348

Every human being,
every living creature,
every living thing is sacred.
The all earth is sacred.

349

The soul has no age.

350

The brightness of the sun,
the darkness of night: everything is

*an indivisible part
of the Oneness of Love.*

351

*Unconditional love
is the heart of your heart*

352

*Conflicts in your life are mirrors
of your inner conflicts.
Harmony in your life is the mirror
of your inner harmony.*

353

*Honor the All
in everything, everywhere
and everyday.*

354

*Life is your creation.
Do not blame others
for what is happening in your life.*

355

*Forgiveness doesn't mean
that you have to interact with the
"offender", forgiveness is an inner act
of healing freedom.*

356

Love and faith are the engines of life.

357

*The world is neither good nor bad.
Don't judge it, just love it.*

358

*Through the mind and judgment,
it is not possible to understand
oneself and others. True understanding
is a compassionate heart.*

359

*Every emotional wound
is due to a lack of love.
Love is the cause and the remedy.
Love is always the answer.*

360

*The past exists
only when we think on it.*

361

Forgive yourself if you want

to be forgiven by others.

362

***You** are responsible for everything
that happens in your life:
responsible but not guilty.*

363

*Never give up. Do it for yourself,
do it for all the people
who can be inspired by you.*

364

***S**mile, when you want to smile.
Cry, when you want to cry.
Perfection is not to be always happy,
perfection is to be always yourself.*

365

You are never alone.
Your Higher Self and your Angels
always whisper to your heart.
By silencing your mind,
you can be filled with their Love.

Other books by Human Angels

We Are Human Angels
The 7 keys to overcome the ego and the 7 keys to live with the heart in service to the Oneness

"*We Are Human Angels*" is the book that has inspired the Human Angels' community around the world.

One year after its publication, this book has already become a global phenomenon and has been spontaneously translated into many other languages by the readers.

"*We Are Human Angels*" is an uplifting guide that leads you, step by step, in your healing journey from overcoming the ego until the fulfillment of your true nature as a Human Angel, in your life and in society. It will help you, both in a spiritual and a practical fashion, to achieve fulfillment in your romantic relationships and also in becoming a better person, ready to help those you see suffering around you.

Do you have an out of the ordinary sensitivity?
Do you have a special talent when it comes to helping others?
Do you feel you are a Human Angel?
This book is for you!

"We Are Human Angels" is available on all major online bookstores. You can read this book in many different languages, either on your e-reader and also in paperback.
All information about the book, the stores and the translations can be found on the official book site:
www.wearehumanangels.com

365 Mantras for Today
Heal your life. Awaken the Human Angel within yourself. Awaken the Divine you.

"What I resist, persists. What I accept, flows".

"*365 Mantras for today*" is a collection of some of the most inspiring quotes that the authors have posted, over the last four years, on their famous Facebook page "We are Human Angels". Their Mantras, which have already helped many people in finding their own path to happiness, will lovingly guide you in your everyday life journey.

"*365 Mantras for today*" goes much further than simply motivational mantras: it is a source of inspiration and a guide that enlightens those moments of your life in which you need inspiration, or when you have to make wise and positive decisions. Thanks to this book, you do not have to climb a mountain, or walk barefoot trough the surf to draw inspiration for your everyday life: just pick up this book and open it at a random page and you will find Your mantra for the day. This is how synchronicity works (and these mantras are based on synchronicity), it is not by chance that you are now reading this book's description. Things always happen for a reason: you were probably looking for *"365 Mantras for today"* although you did not know it.

Awaken the human angel within yourself!

"365 Mantras for today" is available on all major online bookstores, either as an ebook and in paperback.

This book is now also available in Portuguese under the title *"365 Mantras para Hoje"* and German under the title *"365 Mantras Tag für Tag."* This book is currently being translated into many other languages. For news and updates, stay tuned with us!

All information about this book can be found on the book's official page: www.wearehumanangels.com/365-mantras-for-today.

About the Authors

You will not find our names as we have chosen to pen our books as Human Angels, a collective identity that transcends our individuality and belongs to all those who have chosen to live with Unconditional Love in the Oneness.

We have written our books driven by the desire to share our healing journey, a trip through the illusions of the ego to our rebirth in the Oneness.

We have transmuted our experiences into Awareness and Love with the help of powerful, channeled energies that have, increasingly, guided and enlightened the path of our journey.

Meet us on Facebook at the page: We Are Human Angels
www.facebook.com/We-Are-Human-Angels
Twitter: @HUMAN_ANGELS
Website: www.wearehumanangels.com

Text revision: Ross Wilkins
wilkins.ross@rocketmail.com
*Thanks to Ross for assisting us
with so much love and patience*

Contents

p.   9 *Wisdom Pills Leaflet*
p. 13 *365 Wisdom Pills*
p. 115 *Other books by Human Angels*
p. 119 *About the Authors*

Made in the USA
Middletown, DE
21 November 2017